The Umbrella Girl

Not that any drop I wasted

GAYATHRI AGP

notionpress
.com

INDIA · SINGAPORE · MALAYSIA

ISBN 979-8-89632-813-1

The Umbrella Girl

It's All in Me
It's All in Me
How I see Myself
And You
Why go away
Apart.... too far
Too close....too near
Too much to hold
When You go
It's All in Me & You
When You go too close
Too far.... Too near
It's All in Me & You
Together....
When You go this far
This far....this far....this far.....there

The Umbrella Girl

Y: Never thought it's You

X: How well then did You think it's not me

Y: Swear, I saw Myself in You

X: Oh great, ! i am so as I am, Never been You

Y: Believe me, Trust me, I speak the Truth

X: Umh... I know, I heard, but I live in dreams,

Not all that, that come true

Y: I'm dead by last October, did You not miss me

X: Oh gravure, I led a month before, were You behind me

The Dead in Revival

The Umbrella Girl

Caught on the Cam–Era

A tree borne a fruit

The fish swam around

Jona prayed God

The fruit be brought by the fish

And be given to her

God said " Wait, I'm still

Under the Tree"

The Umbrella Girl

Fore- Leaves Knot

Slender Pot of flaute

Flowers drooped in leaves

Amidst the tall grasses kept

What cometh forth fragile

The Buds supple in petals

The Umbrella Girl

(Contd...)
I sat down on the branches,
Relishing the fruits of it
While I see You nectar
The flowers of it, I know,
I have only My legs to climb
Are You A Butterfly &
Never were You
A Caterpillar
Climb, Crawl, in Perch....

The Umbrella Girl

Becoming my Life in Heaven
Fused to me forgetting in stares
Let the Spring come...
The flowers held in emerald
The Heart held in ASap tree
The Shadows bowed in rings
Even the Soul in Her Shelter
Thou Holiness worthy in crores
To live all the births together
She spreads Her wings To relate...

The Umbrella Girl

Let the Spring come (&)

Let the Heart melt while

The frosted clouds blew

& droops the lovely melodies

The Moon on the Move touches

All the love laden Kinsman streets

Sung and taken on procession

Let the Spring come

Dreams heaved upon the daunting

Eyes of mermaids

Found Soulful together

The Heart pounds in a New langue

Lent in Her language Owned

Becoming Mine & in a Bond

Gayathri AGP

The Umbrella Girl

(Contd...)
I sat down on the branches,
Relishing the fruits of it
While I see You nectar
The flowers of it, I know,
I have only My legs to climb
Are You A Butterfly &
Never were You
A Caterpillar
Climb, Crawl, in Perch....

The Umbrella Girl

The Childe & the Caterpillar
Crawl over the branches bow
Unweary of the heights below
What in You that gave You wings
When I still have my legs
Only to climb, i know
It's You & Me
That crawl over the Bow,
WOW, how in You
Came the colors make you fly
Over, I still crawl and I have
My legs only to climb

The Umbrella Girl

Let the Spring come (&)

Let the Heart melt while

The frosted clouds blew

& droops the lovely melodies

The Moon on the Move touches

All the love laden Kinsman streets

Sung and taken on procession

Let the Spring come

Dreams heaved upon the daunting

Eyes of mermaids

Found Soulful together

The Heart pounds in a New langue

Lent in Her language Owned

Becoming Mine & in a Bond

The Umbrella Girl

Becoming my Life in Heaven

Fused to me forgetting in stares

Let the Spring come…

The flowers held in emerald

The Heart held in ASap tree

The Shadows bowed in rings

Even the Soul in Her Shelter

Thou Holiness worthy in crores

To live all the births together

She spreads Her wings To relate…

The Umbrella Girl

(Contd...)
She would happily call both
PAPPA
For one believes it to be Baby
The revered, as the Father
In what so, Annamol remains
A DAUGHTER

The Umbrella Girl

AnnaMol
The most Revered Father
and the father in Heaven
Thou both seek my Annamol
Who Surpassed You both
One receives without
While the Other seeks in form
Not left the Mind, Body & Spirit
The revered hopes in despair
AnnaMol is well natured
Respects & is considerate to all
She does not despise one
And love the other;

The Umbrella Girl

Do not be disturbed in
Unnecessary thoughts
Think of only
What is Ideal for You

Do only what is necessary
Do only what will keep you happy
Be only with people
Who are good to you
Think wise and be safe
Put ourself first
To help others next
Only when You can

The Umbrella Girl

(Contd...)

I said 'Wait' causing him more pain

And we missed to miss

A Sledge, A Boat, A fur

And a Gintin

Drop them and take these

A Ball of Snow

My shrill & His Pain

And the Snow Ball

What for,

The Umbrella Girl

(Contd...)
It rollsover and becomes
Bigger & Bigger
Not can You hold anymore
Ye, let it be, make me warm
& take me home
Stop adventuring
Give me a ring & a marble sling
For my boy does like to play
Frankly never to miss any

The Umbrella Girl

Never forsake Anybody
Who trusts You
Tell them or show
This is all that is
And Nothing more

Do not anticipate in Your
Misgivings, Do not Give Up
Have confidence in yourself
Before the other

Why worry when You fail
When You know there is
No Pass without A Fail

The Umbrella Girl

(Contd...)
My clothes are not enough
I'm eyeing on the furs
And of the deers around
For some extra comfort
They can aide...

My lover is far ahead &
Crossed the miles before
I took the first steps;
3 yards past
He doesn't look behind

The Umbrella Girl

The Umbrella Girl

A Boat's life Down the Snow
Amidst the figs & pines
The sloppy slopes of snow
Not in sedges but in boats

Halo' Snowpeaks on
Faintly Shines, the rays
Show me a bow of
A sledge tightly roped

I have a gintin, no water
Not thirsty &
No Sweat, I shrill
The icy cold chills my spines

Gayathri AGP

The Umbrella Girl

He checks the pace & does Markings
On the Maps where We are to find
Our treasures together hunted & lost

The boat of the Noah's times Not sunk
For we were never been that close and
the snow doesn't melt into rivers to keep
The Boat from jolting down

' I ' said me to myself' and heard 'Joe'
From a distance, who is it? 'Joe'....
This time given even more strongly
'Come fast, Or We are going to miss'
He held so much in His Hand

The Umbrella Girl

Know your Leader

As much as you know

The Followers

Do not sacrifice

For nothing comes

For sacrifice

No value can level

A sacrifice

Nor can become Another

Trust in People whom You love

Do not despise, give them their space F.R.I.E.N.D.S

The Umbrella Girl

DO NOT
Steal   Snatch   Grab
Lie   Forfeit   Force
Threaten   Indulge   Mar
Boast   Blame   Expect
    Not A Virtue

The Umbrella Girl

Do not force upon yourself
      Anything
Neither on anyone else

Keep track on yourself
Do not be disillusioned
In others mockery

Think and pray to GOD
Or LORD whoever
Helps you in need
And keep you protected

The Umbrella Girl

Trust only what you believe is true
Do not fancy TRUTH
That You do not believe

Take Care and Love Yourself first
And Your Brethren
Who wilfully shares with You

Do not make empty and tall Promises
That You struggle to fulfill

Believe in what You say
And Do only when
You are happy about it

The Umbrella Girl

Your Calling is to the Almighty
Your Lord, Your God, what you Worship, believe in Prayers

The Umbrella Girl

Your Calling is to the Almighty
Your Lord, Your God, what you
Worship, believe in Prayers
Never force anybody to believe in what
You do,they may or may not,
but that is not to worry you
As how your payers are answered
Their prayers too as how they seek
Do not be tempted to do wrong
Do not be frustrated to do what you need to
Do not be irritated when things go wrong
There can always be a way to mend
And to set right

The Umbrella Girl

Situated in the Situation
The Fish's Eye

An Isle is situated surrounding by waters,
The waves gushes in & out, throughout its shores
The situation is so dense and thick
In the thickests with no lane!
Yet a Catamaran awaits it's shore to galore
Sceething the Waves....the thickests, the shores, the waves!
I chose fishing insteadto deploy the nets to feed me
All day, & the dark, in the midst, at the Sunset

The Umbrella Girl

A Lovely Peasant

    Beyond My Capacity

Hare, hare....hare

the Peasant brushes her chisel on the blades

the cricket rickets though faded on the grasses

the chisel begotten the fallen straws

in collection failed to reap the grains...

the Straws, the blades, the chisel...no grains!

The lovely Peasant wandered an extra mile

Hare, hare....hare

Weeding Out in all magnificence

for the yield is not ripe early to bear,

No grains! No reaps! in languish she sought an oxen dome!

Hare, hare...hare

The Umbrella Girl

Know your friends and
Tell them why they mean
So much to you

Express your love of gratitude
Show them where You stand With them

Set your standards and
Know Your limits
Before A Venture

Do not give in
Just to make friends
Without becoming One

The Umbrella Girl

A Riverbed Story
     Timed at night
A Watchful Woodpecker pecked the trunk,
A hole to pepin & until dusky to align within
The pecked pecker pecking still
The river by its side had its bed
Drenched in meadowy grass shoots upright
Though lost their sway in the breeze run aflay...
The bed lay with their tiny budstwirling their find
Up & Down running through the muddled in day,
The night calls it's rest as the lives still go on in a bay
Halloween halos bloom with the Looney Star glitter
Do see some over the riverbed peep
The Shadows spark even in the timely nights

The Umbrella Girl

The Wild Deer in the Wildest Roar

A roar, furore, roar eh, the wild deer

Jumps up & low playing by... Aroar

Why, a lion by its side asleep...

Aroar, furore, roar but only gasped in yawning

The wild deer, aroar, furore, roar, the lion yawn

In meek silence, oh the wild deer !

The deer, the deer oh my dear

What you want the lion to be

You are so wild, the lion fell in silence abeit

Aroar, furore, Roar...

Caught in dreams of the wilderness, the lion

Cuddled more to its sides, while the wild deer kept

A bunch of flowers for the lion so wild in the wilderness

Astray, aroar, furore, roar My deer

The Umbrella Girl

Spicy-ing the Cardamom

Spedup fleeing in greed, thoughts into capture

but in Captivation, ' Your life at risk'

Spedup to acquire more to drink in all that you can have

Risk to the very end ; all set to boom, explode in pieces

Where you don't collect your ashes soaked

When the water contaminated, you don't even get back

yourself, let alone of others

Spedup in haste, your head held high

Not minded of the swollen Sword

Thrash the head down on the ground

As your heart gushes out blood on the thirsty mudpool

At an arm's piercing apart, gory aghast!

The Umbrella Girl

(Contd...)
"I want You lay dead on the floor

where you never rise to live again, never again

In my Presence, thine enemy never come true'

Desi, the grammatoire & the repertoire sunkens

In the deepest of the deep, where I not exist

I do not survive, I do not live, I do not exist

I am nothing, Sign me Up now, for I start living again

In depth, in remorse, in surgence of the deepest

Running low & high, Where am I

Come by, let me in, See the myriad miracles passby,

Never Yours not anymore, The Creator doesn't seek

A Patent, to comply with, to say, You are Unrestricted

The Umbrella Girl

The Lousy Lame and the Belle
D'amie, Over the Beverly Hills
The Dame walks in gait, to a Holy Shrine
On its way She saw a lousy lame intact with a kid
To her chest the lame took the kid & cajoled, then put it
On the ground to run....after a few steps the kid ran back
To the lame,..... The Shrine, The Kid, The Lame
Belle in gaity fortress fought in to the shrine,
The Whisk, The Wasp, The Veil & The Dame
When the Bell struck One the Other Two vanished
As the Dame & the Whisk remain

The Umbrella Girl

Crossed Legs not when i sit

Crossing legs over while only in sleep

Lull me in comfort and keep my pains & pangs away

Crossing legs over to take my burden away

Comfort & convince me of my dreams

When I sweat or in tears running down my cheeks

The pains, & pangs in whom I reconcile

Crossing legs in comfort when I comfort myself

In control where goes me off in dreams

Even strangers digging my grave,

My pains pangs to see, not the Soul to rest in peace

When I'm guided & have woken up in eternity

The Spirits run ablaze; no one a looser

And so how You mend my ways always

Gayathri AGP

The Umbrella Girl

In fond memory of my Daughter Aathirai (a) Mithu

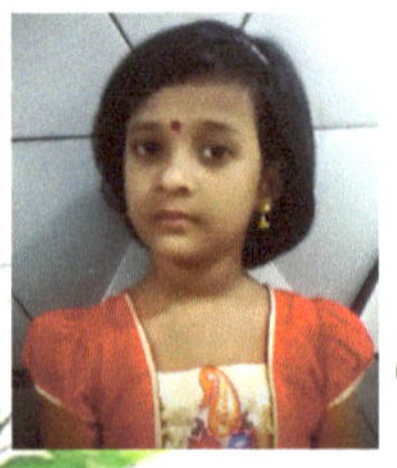
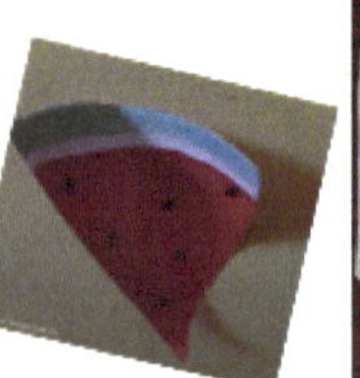

G'agan'YaanAl vu

The Umbrella Girl

Like You, I look into You
For what goes on in my mind
You can see....like you
I see into You, i see, i see
I hear
For what goes on in me
You can hear....like you
I do hear, what in You
Like You, i listen
Never listen to please
Never listen to please
Never listen to please
Listen, for I like You
How You are & what You be

The Umbrella Girl

(Contd...)
Like You, when You don't see
As I don't see You, Like You
For what makes us both
To see the Other in Spirits' Spree
Like You, like You, as I always
Like it to be You

The Umbrella Girl

I did that for You

I yearn, I crave, I beg, it's all that I made

How can I give up when You turn around to ignore

Never said that before, never showed you so

While You led your way For me, I made You

All that I can, nay, how can You reject them right away

Not that I bear, noa proof, nor a spec, how not you care

Neigh, the horse awaits at the door, rise up, and join

For we to go afar fest... Never say No; Never say Yes;

Never say I don't know, Who You are & What I am

I know it's dark that's the reason You don't see me

straight, don't i make sense, Let's do this now

Now that I don't miss You anymore

The Umbrella Girl

The Blind Eye

Gazed with my eyes closed

Gazed with to see the light glow wide awake

Not fallen asleep Gazed and saw them straight

While You stood upright Not in sight

Keep me low, keep me high, keep me whenever I gazed

With my eyes closed, come to say, come in the way

For I gaze with my eyes closed, wat you take

When you spook, for in me I laid, i laid & said

For I gaze with my eyes closed, glow in all you make

To shine & bright for I gaze with my eyes closed

Come to say, Come in the way, Come for the world is

Wide awake, come to say, come in the way, know

The Umbrella Girl

(Contd....)
It's never late,
for I gaze with my eyes closed & know
that You came for me, to say,
that You have come with Your eyes wide awake

The Umbrella Girl

Deadly Sins in deadly silence

Deadly though I feel the Sin

How I may cause you to Sin &

To be Sinned; for You know what it is

And what life is to Sin

Sin, sin when You know & you want to sin

For only you know what is to sin

When You Sin; Who blame whom

For the Sin tells you so 'You have sinned'

Only when they know what it is to sin

In us & in Others; in You & in Me

Why let the other Not just Sin & be Sinned

In Silence, in Sound & in all that You can bound

Sin when you are to know, & you make to know what it is

to Sin & be Sinned, in Silence ever be

The Umbrella Girl

For in sick we surge, do not plunge

Until it's all over far, for far how sick i be

In me I find when I need a search that

Never give in to me, dismayed & crushed

Your hopes to lay, never stand by me, never beside me

For I'm sick and make you weak

Sounds stilth, sounds yappy, crappy

My head goes round where You be, never by my side

Waters Winds shine bright, the feet not on ground

Beseige, lovely though for I'm sick and I make you weak

Never stand by me, never i speak for you

For when I'm sick i make you weak

The Umbrella Girl

The Skies are cloudy and dark & the power shutdown
The mobile survived it's last streaks while a faint drizzle
Outside expected rains on a high, the next two days
instore, i would wait until tomorrow to touch the grounds
To set my eyes & to ponder what would have me done &
To do in silence without pomp, i don't fray & not boast
Of the smiles that don't fade away, am not good in Math
But never shall let my eyes closed if only I have to see
again for all the good souls have goneby
There are fewer occassions when lotus blossom under
the Sun and the lillies under the Moon; With You not so
As you Do carry both, in their fragrances descends moses
afresh and anew

The Umbrella Girl

Pet-ed and fate-d
For the Bow, Vow, Wow !
Gleaming, Sharpy, sniffer
Sweat on its bay
While it's friend trolls all day
Yappy, Crappy, Snoopy
Nothing to interest however gaffy
Laughy jitsy nor sickens the Dickens
From the BackRow
Gather after a hard day
To dither while so much love is not enough to display
Wither all no more pages in tatters, crumbling at
The slightest touch, how much to hold, strange, serene, iQ
The dogs bark, do you hear them from the Books Closet
References in Referendum, i can hear it say
'You are a Nut' , the Pet is clever and it cracked You well

The Umbrella Girl

The rose petals spread in unison, while the actual
Flower sought is a Lotus that is stoned & stands sturdy
For Unity & Integrity; Politics aside, i only speak of the
Quality of a flower found in nature, supple, soft, soles &
souls stems deep into waters, only as the buds, the blooms
Afloat in such fragility, how to trail this, when You stand
In opposition, make a Connect when the differences are
So high, i align only with a few, if to see in other than
mine, i would not have come this far too near
I would fetch without the slightest clue to You
And be Somewhere around without You see
Ever as a journal on Your Street Walls

The Umbrella Girl

A Man claimed in a social context belonging

To a certain period in history,

When I happen to loose one tooth, my opponent,

Who made me loose a tooth should also loose one of His

On another period in history as times passed,

A man claimed in a social context

When I happen to loose one of my teeth, my opponent

Who made me loose may have to loose even more

Than one of his tooth, as my tooth if spared could

Made me realise so much in abundance and of which

I could have made so much of it, of them i could have

Given so much more of it to others. So now that I happen

To loose one tooth, my opponent may have to loose even

more than that of one

 Gayathri AGP

The Umbrella Girl

(Contd...)
Times passed in history,
A Man claimed in a social context belonging to a certain
period, I have happened to loose one of my tooth
i know not how it happened , there is another person
facing me He doesn't know if He had lost anything
at all neither He knew that I have lost a tooth,
not know how
How to claim, the reply was,
' See if You can mend & fend YOurself '

The Umbrella Girl

The Success & the lures of them

Some buddies thought, what I did not know a millennial

years that You can be trained to be a Braveheart;

a Warrior; a Soldier; a Protector; a Guardian; a Saviour

Who entrusts You and to become

While all intricacies known and the unknown explored,

discovered, invented, innovated and to set on fore

to ground underneath or above the skies, some had

weird times mustering up all courage and getting excited

All the runs on their way dwelled, delivered and

reemerging from ardent adventures. They brought great

energies bringing several more wonders where everyone

could rejoice in the success of them

So allured, while All wronged seen to be wrong made to

wrong, now what wrong can make good of it

To compensate a 'good' for it – Do you need someone

to give you work – without knowing what you need

to work for....